ANCIENT BOATS

Because of the difficulty of travelling by land,
from very early times boats were important.
They were made in different ways.

MAKING A LOG BOAT

TRAVELLING SCOTLAND
A Story of Transport

ACTIVITY BOOK

By Ian Morrison
Illustrated by Olwyn Whelan

Edinburgh : HMSO
National Museums of Scotland

TYTLER'S BALLOON

SCOTTIE BOOKS

NOT AN EASY LAND FOR WHEELS

As the bird's-eye view on the inside cover shows, even Scotland's so-called Lowlands are full of hills, the Highlands are strewn with deep lochs, much of the coastal land is cut into by great arms of the sea, and many of the communities are scattered on islands.

So Scotland has never been an easy land to get around on wheels at any period. For centuries, most travellers walked, rode, used pack-animals or went by boat.

SEE HOW MANY DIFFERENT KINDS OF TRANSPORT WITH AND WITHOUT WHEELS YOU CAN DRAW

SKIN-COVERED BOAT   **DUGOUT LOG BOAT**   **PLANK-BUILT BOAT**

Boats on plates can make nice decorations. Get
a paper plate and use colour markers to draw
any of the boats you like from this book onto it.
Perhaps you could add a border of fish and
seashells round the rim, or even an octopus!
(Yes, they do live in the seas around Scotland.)

5

SEAWAYS AND RIVERS

With the development of boats and ships, people could take advantage of the water routes offered by Scotland:
– the rivers and lochs reaching far inland;
– the seaways, which became links between islands rather than barriers, and also allowed trade with distant lands.

A thousand years ago, Vikings (below) were using the Scottish Northern and Western Isles as stepping stones on their seaways.

ICELAND

FAROES

VIKINGS

Five hundred years ago, merchants (below) from the East Coast ports were busy trading across the North Sea.

SHETLAND

NORTH SEA

ORKNEY

HEBRIDES

MERCHANTS

OVERLAND ON FOOT AND HOOF

In the long centuries when Scotland had few roads suitable for wheeled traffic, if they couldn't get there by water, people and their animals simply had to walk, often carrying goods on their backs.

In the 17th and 18th centuries, drovers walked herds of cattle from all over the Highlands to the Falkirk Tryst (a market) and then far south into England. When they had sold the cattle, the men often stayed on to earn more money by working on the English harvest.

Their cattle-herding dogs were not needed for this, so they sent them back north. The dogs were expert at finding their own way home. They called in at the same inns used on the journey south, because their masters had paid in advance for their homeward-bound suppers!

Modern roads and railways often have to follow the same valleys that the old cattle drovers used. Look at the map to see whether your family has used routes which did this, when you were travelling on holiday in Scotland.

Old drove roads converging on Falkirk

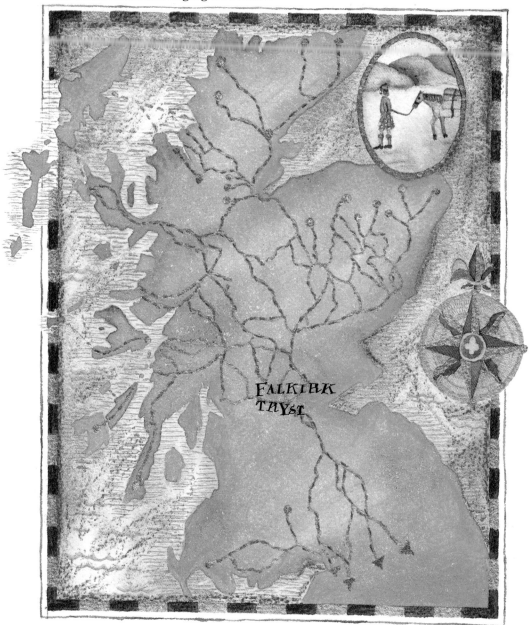

FALKIRK
TRYST

DROVERS AND REIVERS

Reivers were cattle thieves – the first aim of the game is to get your cattle safely to market, then your dogs can race home on their own.

You'll need a coin to toss (heads: two moves; tails: one) and a counter (make one for each player from cardboard) to show where you have got to. Draw a drover (YOU!) on the top of each counter, with your dog on the other side.

START

YOUR HOMES START AND FINISH FOR DOGS

WISELY FORECASTED BAD WEATHER GO STRAIGHT TO INN 2

WOLVES! GO BACK ONE MOVE

CATTLE STILL WILD WAIT 2 TURNS TO SETTLE THEM

LANDSLIDE AT PASS DELAYS BY 1 TURN

LOCH

INN 1

WAIT 2 TURNS UNTIL REIVERS GIVE UP AMBUSH

DARE YOU TAKE THE SHORT CUT!

DI A. STE... GO STA...

Use the top side for the outward trip, then turn the counters over for the dogs to run home.

Now that they don't have the cattle to look after, they don't have to stop for rivers or ambushes, but they need their suppers. You must get the right throw for them to visit each inn, even though this may take up several turns and allow your rivals to overtake your hound.

INN 2

DOG CHASES RABBIT ON THE WAY HOME WAIT 2 TURNS

INN 3

STORM! RIVER DIFFICULT TO CROSS WAIT 2 TURNS

RIVER STILL HIGH WAIT ONE TURN

MARKET

OVERCOMING OBSTACLES

To make it easier to travel, people have put a lot of effort into overcoming Scotland's natural obstacles. They have built roads and railways, replaced fords and ferries with bridges, driven tunnels through mountains and under rivers, and cut canals.

More and more of this has been done in the last three hundred years, but the work started thousands of years ago. For example, in prehistoric times people laid trackways of tree trunks to let them cross dangerous peat bogs that blocked the Forth Valley west of Stirling.

Sometimes what they did served more than one purpose. For example, during World War II, the geography of the Orkney Islands was changed by the building of the Churchill Barriers. These blocked off seaways to keep enemy submarines out of the Scapa Flow anchorage, but also created direct road links between islands, benefiting their communities ever since.

What kinds of things have people done to change the geography of parts of Scotland that your family knows?

Making a prehistoric trackway.

Churchill Barrier in Orkney.

SEE HOW LONG LISTS YOU CAN MAKE OF THINGS THAT WERE DONE
(a) LONG AGO;

(b) QUITE RECENTLY

13

Canals, Navvies and Dredgers

Compared to England, few canals were cut in Scotland, but they changed the geography in bold ways. Even the little Crinan Canal made a real shortcut to the Western Isles.

The Forth–Clyde Canal and the Caledonian Canal provided routes between the North Sea and the Atlantic, which avoided having to go round the north of Scotland. This was important before ships had engines, because sailing ships often had to wait for weeks before they got winds in the right direction to let them sail round the mainland.

The Caledonian Canal was becoming out of date even before it was completed, because steam-power was replacing sails. In fact, from 1807 steam dredgers were used by Thomas Telford (1757 – 1834) to cut the canal, the first time this had been done anywhere in the world. Their development of steam dredging could even be said to have 'made Clydeside'. Clyde-built ships became world famous, but before the upper Clyde was deepened by steam dredgers in the 19th century, cattle could ford the river far downstream from where great battleships and liners were to be launched.

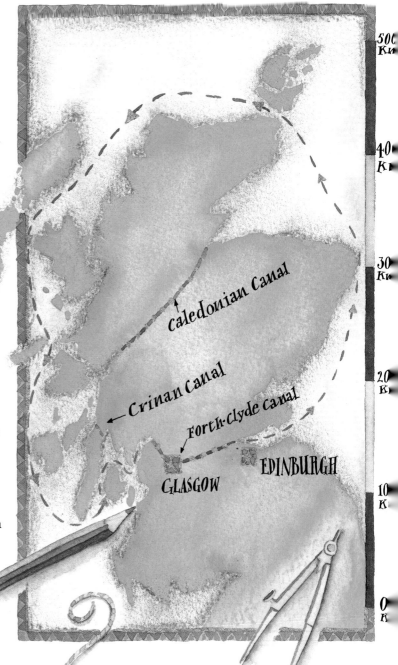

Caledonian Canal

Crinan Canal

Forth-Clyde Canal

GLASGOW

EDINBURGH

500 Km

400 Km

300 Km

200 Km

100 Km

0 Km

Use a piece of string to compare the distances you would have had to go to travel by boat from Edinburgh to Glasgow

a) by the Forth – Clyde Canal;

b) by the Caledonian Canal;

c) by sailing round the north of Scotland.

Use the scale ruler drawn on the map to measure the string each time, if you want to know the distances in kilometres.

Canals were called "Navigations", so the diggers became known as "Navvies".

A steam dredger of Telford's period.

SPEED UNDER SAIL

Cutty Sark

Although the rise of steam-power got underway around two centuries ago, an exciting part of the Great Age of Sail still lay ahead. Engines and coal fuel were expensive, and while some Scots played a leading part in developing steamers, others were among the world leaders in building sailing ships fast enough to race the steamers (and each other!) round the world, for valuable cargoes such as tea from China.

The most famous Tea Clipper of all was *Cutty Sark,* called after the witch in Robert Burns' poem. Built in 1869 at Dumbarton, she may be visited at Greenwich. Later, many Scottish-built clippers fetched Australian wool. One is being conserved at Irvine.

How tea boxes were stowed in Cutty Sark.

It was not just the big sailing ships built by Scots which were fast. Before the steam railway, one of the swiftest ways of commuting between Edinburgh and London was by little Leith sailing cutters. Though these had only one mast, they could carry lots of sails.

SEE IF YOU CAN WORK
OUT WHERE EACH SAIL
WOULD BE SET ON
THE LEITH TO LONDON CUTTER....
THEN HAVE A LOOK AT PAGE 21 TO SEE IF
YOU'VE GOT IT RIGHT!

THE STEAM SHIP COMES

Scots have played an important part in the story of powering transport by steam. Over two hundred years ago, James Watt (1736 – 1819) developed engines that worked more effectively than ever before.

Then in 1803 William Symington (1763 – 1830) made the world's first really effective steam tugboat. His tiny *Charlotte Dundas* pulled barges along the Forth–Clyde Canal, but her paddlewheels kicked up waves which some people thought might undermine the canal banks, so she was not used.

In 1812, however, Henry Bell started the first passenger steamer service in Europe, with the paddler *Comet* plying the Clyde between Glasgow and Greenock.

After that, the development of steamships during last century was in many ways as spectacular as the development of aircraft in this century.

Scotland played a very important part in this. From the 1870s until the start of World War I in 1914, almost one in five of the whole world's ships was 'Clyde-built', and there were other famous shipyards in Aberdeen, Dundee and Leith. They built vessels for all the world's oceans, from the Arctic to the Pacific.

They even made steamers that could be taken apart, and shifted overland to mountain lakes. A delightful example, the *Sir Walter Scott,* still steams around Loch Katrine in the Trossachs Rob Roy country.

The "Sir Walter Scott"

Make yourself a BIG picture of the Comet for your bedroom wall! You will need a piece of paper twice the size of this page. With a soft pencil, rule squares onto it, each 2 centimetres across. Use the squares to help you copy the picture. If you use marker pens for the boat and the people, you can rub out the pencil squares when you have finished.

Eraser!

Paddling from Edinburgh to Aberdeen

The paddle steamer *Brilliant* opened up the Edinburgh – Aberdeen passenger steamer service. She was built in the 1820s.

Has your family ever travelled by sea?
Could you draw a ship they have been aboard?

Make a list of differences between present-day ferries and the one below.
- *What moves them?*
- *What cargo do they carry?*
- *What do the crews have to do?*
- *What is it like for families travelling as passengers?*

The Brilliant.

LEITH~LONDON CUTTER →

Were you right in solving the puzzle (PAGE 17) about where the sails were set?

THE PUFFERS

Some of the most famous ships built in Scotland were huge – like the *Queen Mary*, and the two *Queen Elizabeth*s.

But some of the most beloved steamers were tiny – these were the puffers, designed to fit into the locks of the canals. Until well into the present century they roamed the seaways of the Western Isles, delivering whatever was needed, from coal to bathtubs. They didn't even need to have a proper harbour. A puffer could sit down on her flat bottom on a sandy beach, to be unloaded into a crofter's cart when the tide went out.

Heads to go to the lighthouse

Tails again?

Throw 2 heads before sheep get caught.....

SUNK by the Whirlpool! You needed Heads to escape......

Atlantic Storm Shelter here for 2 turns.

Quick stop: move on 3

Island Wedding: miss 3 turns!

Wait 2 turns for low tide, to unload on beach.

canal busy wait 2 turns

Puffers!

You have to deliver a cargo to a Hebridean island, and get back to your home port. As in the Drovers game, you'll need a coin to toss (heads: two moves; tails: one; remember?) and a cardboard counter for each player. This time, make them in the shape of little puffers, with a different colour for each player. *counters.*

HOME PORT!

STAR T and FINISH

FASTER OVERLAND

In the 19th century, land transport as well as water transport was developing very rapidly in Scotland. At the start of the century, new roads were allowing faster horse-drawn traffic, including stage coaches and mail coaches run to tight schedules.

Station Omnibus

Royal Mail Stage Coach

THE CRAIGIE VAN EXPRESS

Even 'person-power' took to wheels when in 1839 a Scot, Kirkpatrick Macmillan (1813 – 78), made one of the first successful cycles driven by pedals. Soon whole platoons of soldiers were to be seen whirling through the streets of Edinburgh on high bicycles, popularly known as 'penny farthings.'

The Craigievar Express (now in the Grampian Transport Museum) was a wondrous home-built steam tricycle. However, a more important application of steam to road transport was to traction engines and steam lorries.

PENNY FARTHING

PAINT YOUR MOBILE!

Make yourself a penny farthing mobile.

Draw it LARGE on a sheet of stiff white card: trace round a soup plate and a jam-jar lid to get the wheels circular.

Then lace the thread as shown...

Use a nail to pierce lots of little holes just inside the tyres, and make a bigger hole in the middle of the wheel.

THE STEAM RAILWAY AGE

Before our present age of the motor car and diesel truck, railways became a vital part of the transport of both people and goods in Scotland. By the 1880s there was an impressive network serving most parts of the country, including many places that cannot be reached by rail today. Just as Scots ended up building ships not only for themselves but for sale elsewhere in the world, so they built steam locomotives. Springburn, by Glasgow, became a leading exporter of locomotives, like Clydeside for ships.

THE WORLD FAMOUS FORTH BRIDGE

SCOTLAND FOR

Services and fares from BRIT

YOUR HOLIDAYS

stations, offices and agencies

OVER THE TOP

Great engineering feats were needed to create the networks of roads and railways which changed our patterns of movement away from the use of waterways, which had been such an important part of life in Scotland in earlier ages.

The crossing of the Forth is an example of this. For centuries, as the placenames tell, there had been ferry boats sailing between North and South Queensferry. Then in the late 19th century, the great railway bridge was built using the kind of skills that had been learned up to that time. In the 20th century, the shift away from rail to road transport created a great demand for a road bridge. This was built as a 'suspension' bridge, hung from spun cables unlike the 'cantilever' rail bridge, by methods unavailable to the earlier engineers.

Do you know what a CANTILEVER bridge is? Benjamin Baker, the designer of the Forth Rail Bridge, explained that it just means something that sticks out like a shelf or veranda – unlike a SUSPENSION bridge that is hung from cables.

Did You Know?

THE FORTH RAIL BRIDGE is Great Britain's longest CANTILEVER BRIDGE. Its two main spans are 521 m (1710ft) long.

Britain's longest railway bridge, of any kind, is also in Scotland. The present Tay Bridge is 3552 m (11,653ft) long. Of its 85 spans, 74 with a length of 3136m (10,289ft) are over the river.

The railway track of the Forth Rail Bridge is 47.5 m (156 ft) above the water surface.

Britain's highest railway bridge is slightly higher than the Forth Rail Bridge and also in Scotland. It was built even earlier – it is the Ballochmyle viaduct over the River Ayr, 51.5 m (169 ft) over the river.

The Forth Rail Bridge was started in November 1882, and officially opened in March 1890. About four thousand five hundred men worked on it; 57 were killed.

A century later, the Forth Rail Bridge is still making records. When HRH Prince Edward switched on over 1000 floodlights, connected by 40 kilometres (25 miles) of cable, in 1992, it became the biggest illuminated bridge in the world.

Now, in the 1990s, 200 trains cross the Forth Rail Bridge in 24 hours, carrying 14.5 million tons and 3 million passengers in a year.

THE FORTH ROAD BRIDGE may not be the biggest SUSPENSION BRIDGE in the world, but it is quite a worthy partner to the Forth Rail Bridge.

It took 300 men three and a half years to build, and was opened in September 1964.

Its towers are 150 m, (492 ft) tall, and 39,000 tons of steel were used.

Each of the main cables stretches 2134 m (7000 ft) from anchorages in concrete-plugged tunnels driven deep into the rock of the north and south shores of the Forth.

These cables, just 0.6m (2ft) in diameter, get their strength from being spun from lots of thin (5 mm, 0.2 inch) wires made of rust-proof steel.

There are around 145 acres of paintwork with five coats to do, and it can take 10 years to work right across, and then it is time to start again......

Getting Around Town

Industry developed fast in the 19th century. This led to a great growth of Scotland's cities. Transport systems grew to cope with this expansion – suburban railways, both on the surface and also, in Glasgow, underground; horse-drawn buses and tramcars, and later on electric trams and trolley buses, and motor buses. The first motor bus service was in Edinburgh in 1898, the next was in Falkirk.

Horse-drawn Tramcar

THEN and NOW How many modern vehicles can you draw that do the same jobs as the old ones shown here?

GLASGOW DISTRICT SUBWAY

ROUND THE CITY IN HALF AN HOUR

THE ONLY UNDERGROUND CABLE RAILWAY IN THE WORLD. NO SMOKE. NO STEAM. PERFECT VENTILATION. CABLE SPEED FIFTEEN MILES AN HOUR. 2½ MINUTES STATION TO STATION.

FARE, 1d. AND 2d., ACCORDING TO DISTANCE. NO NEED FOR TIME TABLES, TRAINS EVERY FEW MINUTES, WITH PERFECT REGULARITY. ROOMY AND COMMODIOUS CARS.

London didn't start until the next year.

Before there were motor taxis, horse-drawn cabs were for hire.

Businesses and families had private horse-drawn vehicles of many kinds, just as today they have petrol- and diesel-powered trucks, vans and cars.

The Coming of the Car

In the earlier part of this century, some exciting cars were designed and built in Scotland, but comparatively few Scottish families owned a car of their own until after the 1950s. Since then, the great increase in private cars has made it more and more difficult to keep public transport going at a reasonable cost, despite the importance of train and bus services to people without cars in rural and urban areas.

Though more and more Scots have cars, these have mostly come from the giant foreign corporations, and the small Scottish car industry has faded away, like the once much larger ship and locomotive building industries.

Galloway 1924

Arrol Johnston 1906

Argyll 1907

Albion Dog Cart

The
reign
[D]aimler
[1]898:
[t]he first
[pe]trol-powered
[ho]rseless
[ca]rriage in
[Du]nfermline

Simpson Steam Car

WORDSEARCH

Find the names of five Scottish car makers

T	O	A	D	H	A	L
A	A	C	E	U	L	S
R	R	A	E	R	B	I
B	O	R	R	R	I	M
A	L	G	G	I	O	P
R	J	Y	A	C	N	S
R	O	L	L	A	D	O
E	H	L	L	N	O	N
L	N	B	O	E	G	S
R	S	A	W	T	C	T
O	T	G	A	Y	A	E
A	O	P	Y	P	R	A
D	N	I	O	H	T	M
H	Z	P	H	O	P	C
O	W	E	N	N	R	A
G	I	N	N	E	E	R

L E M M I N G ⚡ P R E S S E S

SCOTT IE

THE EARLIEST AERONAUTS

Aviation started early in Scotland! What must have been one of the first-ever attempts at hang gliding took place around 1500, when a man called Damian, who had been pretending he could turn lead into gold, tried to flee from the wrath of the Scots court at Stirling Castle by leaping from the ramparts in a feather suit.

In 1784 James Tytler (1745 – 1804) made the first-ever hot-air balloon flight in Great Britain, at Orchardbrae in Edinburgh. He was laughed at by the locals, but congratulated by Vicenzo Lunardi (1759 – 1806), an intrepid Italian balloonist who made several gas balloon flights in Scotland in 1785. These inspired Robert Burns to write his poem 'Tae a Louse', about the beastie crawling over Missie's fine 'Lunardi Bonnet'– the balloon-shaped hat she was wearing in kirk to show off that she was one of the admirers who had sewn his cloth balloon for him!

AHHGH!

DAMIAN IN A FEATHER SUIT

TYTLER'S BALLOON

VICENZO LUNARDI

35

HIGHLAND AIR

A De Havilland Dragon Rapide in Barra 1946

Proper aircraft have been designed and built in Scotland – not least the Prestwick Pioneer and Twin Pioneer. They were used from the Arctic to tropical jungles, because they could fly from short rough airstrips. These Scottish aircraft are no longer made, but the ability to use grass fields and even land on the beach when the tide is out (in the puffer tradition) is still valuable in linking scattered Scottish communities. Little aircraft act as air ambulance, post-bus and indeed school bus.

This is nothing new – the difficult geography of so much of Scotland for land transport encouraged the development of air services to the Highlands and Islands from the 1930s onwards, using biplanes at first. In recent years, Sumburgh in Shetland has sometimes been the busiest helicopter airfield in the world. Why? Because the North Sea oil workers are taken out to the off-shore rigs.

POST BAG

Biplane means 'with two sets of wings' (top and bottom). In which of these words does 'bi-' mean 'two', and in which does it not? (Clue: in six it does) (Answers on page 40)

See how long a list you can make of words where 'bi-' means 'two'. Use a dictionary if you like!

BIAS BICENTENARY
BIFF BICYCLE
BIGAMY BIFOCAL
BILLION BIMETALLIC
BILIOUS BINGO BIPED
BISON BIZARRE BISHOP

TRANSPORTS OF DELIGHT

Down the ages Scots have enjoyed themselves
by getting around in all sorts of different ways:

How many ways can you spot here?
How many MORE can YOU think of?

HANG GL[IDER]

MOTORBIKE

BOAT

Doon the Watter, Broomielaw

BALLOON

PLACES TO VISIT AND ANSWERS

Transport Museums

General

Myreton Motor Museum,
Aberlady, East Lothian (087 57) 288

Grampian Transport Museum &
Railway Museum,
Alford, Aberdeenshire (033 983)635

Royal Museum of Scotland,
Chambers Street, Edinburgh
(031) 225 7534

Summerlee Heritage Park,
West Canal Street, Coatbridge,
Strathclyde (0236) 31261

Museum of Transport,
Kelvin Hall, 1 Bunhouse Road,
Glasgow
(041) 357 3929

Aviation

Museum of Flight,
East Fortune Airfield, near North
Berwick, East Lothian (062 088) 308

Dumfries & Galloway Aviation
Museum,
The Control Tower, Heathhall
Industrial Estate, Dumfries, Tel Mr
Reid (0387) 59546

Railways

Bo'ness & Kinneil Railway,
The Station, Union Street, Bo'ness,
West Lothian (0506) 822298

Motor Vehicles

Doune Motor Museum,
Doune, Perthshire (0786) 841203

Glenluce Motor Museum,
Glenluce, Newton Stewart,
Wigtownshire (05813) 534

Maritime

Aberdeen Maritime Museum,
Provost Ross's House, Shiprow,
Aberdeen (0224) 585788

Shetland Museum,
Lower Hillhead, Lerwick (0595)5057

Scottish Maritime Museum,
Laird Forge, Gottries Road, Irvine,
Strathclyde (0294) 78283

RRS Discovery and Museum
Discovery Point
Dundee (0382) 201 245

Scottish Fisheries Museum
Harbour Head
Anstruther, Fife (0333) 310 628

Bicycles

Scottish Cycle Museum,
Drumlanrig Castle, Thornhill,
Dumfriesshire (0848) 31555

Forth Bridges

Queensferry Museum,
Council Chambers, South
Queensferry
(031) 331 1590

Answers

Page 32: Wordsearch

T	O	A	D	H	A	L	L
A	A	C	E	U	L	S	E
R	R	A	E	R	B	I	M
B	R	R	R	R	I	M	M
A	O	G	G	I	O	P	I
R	L	Y	A	C	N	S	N
R	J	L	L	A	D	O	G
E	O	L	L	N	O	N	E
L	H	B	O	E	G	S	X
R	N	A	W	T	C	T	P
O	S	G	A	Y	A	E	R
A	T	P	Y	P	R	A	E
D	O	I	O	H	T	M	S
H	N	P	H	O	P	C	S
O	Z	E	Y	O	R	A	E
G	W	I	N	N	E	R	S

Page 37: 'Bi-' means 'two' in the
following words: bicentenary, bicycle,
bifocal, bigamy, bimetallic, biped